TEXAS
BARBECUE 101

By JOHN LOPEZ aka Chef Wally
Foreword by Jerry Flemmons

Great Texas Line Press
Fort Worth, Texas

Cover photographs by Ralph Lauer
Cover barbecue smoked by Pat Craine
Illustrations by Jackie Avila

Bulk sales of books from Great Texas Line Press are available at special disounts
for fundraising, promotions and premiums.
Great Texas Line Press
Post Office Box 11105
Fort Worth, Texas 76110
1-800-73-TEXAS/FAX 817-926-0420
Email: greattexasline@hotmail.com
Visit our website to see our full line of Texas books www.greattexasline.com

ACKNOWLEDGMENTS

I would like to thank a few people for helping me put this boo
together:

My partner and wife, Princess Kathi, for putting up with my gettin
up at all hours of the night to tend a fire, for being the world's be:
dishwasher and sidekick, and for her undying support for me and m
effort.

My daughter Kim and son-in law Kevin, for being the official br
ket critics and tasters.

My grandson Ellis, for being wonderful and inspiring.

My father, Jesse, for teaching me to appreciate barbecue, for taki
me along to the great barbecue joints in the '50s and '60s and for pa
ing on the "hole-in-the-ground" method of cooking barbecue that
father taught him.

My sister, Kathy, for saving, using and sharing Mom's recipes.

My mother, Doris, who spent her life showing us the way.

I dedicate this book to these folks. It is because of them I was
to write this book.

I would also like to thank my publisher, Barry Shlachter, for
sessing the patience of Job.

– John Lopez, aka Chef

TABLE OF CONTENTS

FOREWORD
On Texas Barbecue

By Jerry Flemmons

Of the world's great cuisines — French, Italian, Chinese and Texan — only the latter has a recipe beginning, "First, dig a three-foot hole …"

The idea here is to fill the hole with a dense, hot-burning wood like, say, mesquite; reduce it to fiery coals; spread a thin layer of dirt over the coals; lay in burlap-wrapped chunks of beef; cover with more dirt; then go do something else for 24 hours.

Dig up the beef, and there you have it: Texas barbecue. The real thing.

This classic recipe is straight from historic Texas culinary records and the prairies on which the art of barbecuing began. Let's review the simple historical facts:

Texas foods, jazz, jeans and Elvis souvenirs are the only true American art forms, recognizable around the world.

For the record, Texas invented the margarita, frozen steak fingers, stadium nachos, the marpeani (a regular martini with the olive replaced by a black-eyed pea), the flour tortilla (the DNA building block of entire fast-food empires), chili, corn chips and that most succulent of American dishes, the magnificent Lucullan feast of the plains — heavy beef barbecue.

Early Spanish explorers took an Indian word — barbacoa — to explain closed-pit cooking. By the mid-19th century, when chuck-wagon cooks were using this method to tenderize and flavor tough Longhorn beef, the term had become … barbecue.

There you have it: Texas invented barbecue.

Here in more modern times, the science has changed very little. Today, the "oven" is often of brick or adobe or black-painted steel, and the beef is often a large prime-cut brisket massaged with a spicy dry rub, sometimes bathed in a mopped-on sauce and left to cook for as long as 24 hours over a low heat from a hardwood fire, which produces smoke that envelops — permeates — the meat. It's no great mystery. A closed oven, patience and smoke cause barbecue, and, done right, the meat can be flaked with a fork.

Understand that Texas barbecue is not one of those gimmicky dishes trotted out to feed the tourists, like Hawaiian poi or Alabama grits. It is a daily fare across the state. There are upwards of two thousand barbecue outlets — joints — in Texas, and within most of them there is a generalized ritual to the meal:

The meat is sliced cross-grain and thick, and only in sissy places is the fat trimmed off. On the side, there can be pinto beans, coleslaw, potato salad, an always-secret sauce (either lathered on the meat or served in a dish for sopping), jalapeño peppers, raw white onions, dill pickles, slices of white bread, iced tea or longneck beer and, for dessert, choices of banana pudding, fruit cobbler or pecan pie.

In traditional joints, the only menu probably is scribbled on a blackboard, the beef is served on sheets of butcher paper, seating is at long bare wooden tables (or perhaps old picnic tables outside), the walls are streaked with years of smoke and the clientele ranges from expensively suited professionals to jeaned and booted cowpokes to longhaired wanderers to matrons taking a shopping break. The eating of barbecue is a societal leveler, a classless event. They are all there to eat beef, and just beef.

Just beef. And there's the problem. Almost anything can be barbecued using the patented Texas method. South Texans do a credible job with baby goat (cabrito, it's called). I once sampled barbecued possum (it tasted like chicken, but not enough), and I've seen baloney listed on an Arkansas BBQ menu. Barbecued baloney. My lord.

It's far easier to explain what Texas barbecue is not. It's not shredded pork with peppers, as North Carolinians sell in goldfish cartons. "Texas barbecue is never pork," raged Griffin Smith Jr. to a national audience in the March 1975 edition of *The Atlantic*.

Mr. Smith is correct, but the South is slow in understanding this simple truth. When the secret of Texas barbecue jumped the Magnolia Wall and spread eastward, barbecue, for reasons none of us out here understand, became … pork and other pig stuff. I tasted it once. It's … mushy, not firm and tasty like real barbecued beef. I had to wash out my mouth with a Dr Pepper.

I have a friend, a professional barbecue cook, who thinks the "pork plague" (as he calls it) happened because Tennesseans, Carolinians, Alabamans and Georgians cannot tell a cow from a pig.

Let me explain one more time: The cow, the only source of beef, from which real Texas barbecue is only made, is the one without the curly tail. You could look it up.

PUBLISHER'S NOTE: *Since playwright-author-journalist Jerry Flemmons wrote this essay for* Southern Living *(reprinted here by permission of Chris Flemmons, his son), Texans have embraced pork ribs as well as some other exotic critters for smoking purposes. This cultural shift was not the fault of our author, himself a proud native Texan, but because of it he has included some choice non-beef recipes in this book. We hope the late and much lamented Mr. Flemmons will not be restless in his grave as a result.*

GETTING STARTED

Introduction: Texas Barbecue 101

Ahhhhhhh, the aroma … yeah, the aroma … that's it. It's the aroma that makes my mouth water and my heart skip a beat. The anticipation of chowing down on Texas barbecue almost puts me in a trance. That first wisp of smoke is an assault on my olfactory senses and a huge natural appetite-enhancer. Someone hand me a drool cup.

Hi, I'm Chef Wally. I have been barbecuing for over 35 years and have come to appreciate and practice the fine art and science of Texas barbecue. Sure, there's barbecue in places besides Texas, but that barbecue pales in comparison to the tasty treats that come off barbecue pits in the Lone Star State. I will show you how to cook Texas barbecue for your family and friends

Let's begin by defining what Texas barbecue is and what it isn't. Grilling, for example, is a great way to cook food fast and make it taste good — but grilling is not barbecue, at least not in Texas. I will not show you how to grill in this little book.

What is Texas barbecue? Texas barbecue is dominated by beef — beef brisket, beef clods, beef ribs and sirloin, to name a few — though we Texans also enjoy our pork, fowl, lamb and goat, and you will often find some of those meats at the most authentic of Texas barbecue joins.

Texas barbecue is made up of two basic styles of cooking; East Texas style and Central Texas style. There are other ways to cook Texas barbecue, but these two styles dominate the Texas barbecue map.

East Texas style: Pitmasters cook the meat for a very long time with low, smoky heat, usually less than 210 degrees F. Hickory, oak and mesquite are the fuels most often used, and the meats are turned out with a very smoky flavor. The pits usually have a firebox connected to one end of the pit; the meat is at the other end, and temperature is regulated by controlling the air flow in and out of the pit. East Texas barbecue fans prefer this style of barbecue's intense smoky flavor.

Central Texas style: The first step in this style is to allow hardwood to burn down to embers; mesquite and oak are popular fuels. Instead of a firebox at one end of the pit and the meat at the other, Central Texas style places the meat on a grill above the burning embers, with more vertical distance from the fire than in the East Texas style. Cooking temperature is regulated by moving the meat further from or closer to the fire, or by adding more embers. Central Texas barbecue is often cooked with a higher temperature than in the East Texas style, usually up to 350 degrees F but sometimes even higher. The pits are usually rectangular, about 3 feet high and up to 8 or more feet long, with an opening at one of the bottom ends for the fire. Fans of this style find East Texas barbecue too smoky and prefer the lightly smoked, char-grilled flavor of their efforts.

My style: I have adapted my barbecuing style to produce the tastes I like, so I use a hybrid version of these two styles in my cooking. I like a little more smoky flavor than that of most barbecue cooked in the Central Texas style, but not quite as much smoke as the East Texas style imparts.

This book will show you how to make Texas barbecue in your backyard. You don't have to have a lot of expensive equipment, although your budget is the only limit on what you *could* spend. I've had barbecue from a 55 gallon drum "pit" that was perfect in my eyes, and I have had some less-than-wonderful barbecue that came off an expensive rig.

My Barbecue Belief System is based on simplicity. I don't care for complex barbecue recipes. I use simple, easy-to-find ingredients, a basic Texas smoker-style pit and lots of TLC. I don't like to marinate, as I believe that can mask the flavor of the meat and affect the texture in an adverse way. I don't like to use mops or basting sauces. I don't believe they are necessary, and I don't like opening my pit once I start the cooking process; I try to open my pit only to put meat on, take it off or turn it. On the other hand, I do get great flavor from meats that have been brined, a process that seems to enhance the meat flavor and add moisture.

I don't believe in wrapping barbecue in foil to cook it, as that *steams* the meat and changes the texture in an unfavorable way. I don't want to have my meat "fall off the bone"; I want to chew it off. Perfect texture is a major element of great barbecue. To steal a term from my Italian buddies, "to the tooth," or *al dente*, best describes *my* ideal barbecue.

There are many people who love to marinate, mop and sauce their barbecue. I have had those types of barbecue many times, and they can taste very good. I just prefer the elemental flavors of meat, smoke and a little seasoning.

Enjoy the recipes and keep on barbecuing!

– Chef Wally

What you'll need

There are many variations of pits in the marketplace. There are also many people who find various ways to make their own. I have eaten barbecue from a "modified" U.S. mailbox and an old refrigerator, and I once constructed a makeshift smoker from a galvanized metal garbage can.

I started my barbecue journey with a series of 55-gallon drum pits. If you live in Texas, these are the pits you see for sale in the parking lots of grocery stores. They are inexpensive and with a little care can last five years or more. They are large enough to cook a nice quantity of beef, ribs and sausage. The downside of these pits is that you have to open the whole pit to tend the fire, which causes longer cooking times, fluctuations in temperature and less consistent results. For the money, though, these are a good buy.

From the drum pit, I evolved to the Texas-style offset pit. This is usually made from steel pipe or rolled steel. It has a firebox that is offset from the meat pit. This barbecue pit allows complete control of temperature by adjusting the air flow; look for one with a built-in thermometer in the meat pit. The pit I am using now is 18 inches in diameter and a little more than 3 feet long. The fire box is offset, 18 inches in diameter and about 2 feet long. I believe it to be the right size for

most backyard barbecue cooks, and this is what I most recommend. I can cook two briskets at a time along with some ribs and sausage.

If you need to cook more than this amount on a frequent basis, you will need a larger pit. Fortunately, they come in all sizes.

If you prefer the Central Texas style of barbecuing, you will need a brick, concrete or steel pit 2 to 3 feet wide, 4 to 8 feet long and 3 feet high, with a lid made of steel. This is either a lot more expense or a lot of work to build, but such a pit can last many years and provide lots of barbecue and enjoyment.

Then there is the traditional Texas barbacoa pit: a hole dug in the ground, lined with rocks or bricks, filled with burning embers and your meat of choice, then covered and left to slowly cook the meat for 8 hours or more. (See the Barbacoa recipe on page 36 for more details.)

Now we get to the part where I might rile a bunch of folks. Yes, you can cook barbecue on a kettle cooker, a gas barbecue grill or an electric smoker. I don't use them and don't recommend them. If one of these devices is your choice, for whatever reason, then charge ahead. My idea of barbecue is cooked with coals, embers and/or wood. 'Nuff said.

Barbecue Essentials

You'll want to round up some essential supplies and some tools to make your barbecue job a little easier. Here is my checklist.

Charcoal: Natural lump charcoal is preferred. Avoid easy- or quick-start charcoal and briquettes. These can impart an off odor and/or taste to your barbecue.

Wood: I like to use Texas post oak. I use hickory and mesquite if I have to, but they result in a stronger, more acrid smoke flavor, so tread gently. When I use mesquite, I always wait until it burns down to embers before I add it to my fire.

Tongs: I like 9-inch spring-loaded stainless-steel tongs like those restaurants use; I don't like the locking tongs (although they are easy to store in a drawer). These simple tongs are inexpensive, last a long time and are very effective at picking up, turning and moving your barbecued meats. I keep a pair of tongs at my pit and a few in the kitchen. If 9 inches sounds too short for you, try 12-inch ones.

Charcoal chimney: If I had to choose my "can't live without" tools, I'd pick my charcoal chimney and my 9-inch tongs. The charcoal chimney is a must. You could start a fire with a blowtorch, or you could use an electric starter, but do not use any type of lighter fluid. The fuel can taint your food's aroma and taste.

Mop: If you like to mop or baste, you can buy a kitchen mop of the cotton-strand variety. Trim the strands to about 5 or 6 inches long, cut the handle down to about 12 inches, and you have a great sop mop. If this seems too heavy-duty for you, you can buy a smaller barbecue mop or use a silicone baster. They come in all sizes and colors.

Drip/water pan: You may want to catch the drippings as you cook and/or have a water source in your pit to prevent dryness. Disposable aluminum foil pans are fine, but I use aluminum and stainless baking/roasting pans. Once they go in the pit, you will want them to reside there, as they will get lots of grease and smoke deposits. I try to clean my drip pans every time I start a new batch of barbecue.

Spatula: If you need one for your grill, try to get a restaurant type with large flat blade and handle that is not too long. I find the typical long-handled barbecue tools to be cumbersome.

Thermometers: For testing meat temperatures, you can use an instant-read type, either digital or analog. Some of the more elaborate thermometers have a probe that stays in your meat and can alert you with a signal to a receiver outside the pit when the proper temp is reached. I don't use these, but some of my buddies swear by 'em. For monitoring pit temperature, I have a regular analog-type thermometer mounted in the lid of my pit.

Fire shovel: I use a small fireplace shovel to move coals and embers to my pit. These are inexpensive and can be picked up at your local hardware store.

Meat lifting aids: Heavy-duty grill gloves made from heat-resistant material, such as Pit Mitts, are good tools for handling meat on the pit, as are Meat Claws, a pair of curved "handles" with short prongs on one end for securing the meat and heat-resistant grip handles for lifting on the other.

Barbecue fork: "Don't want 'em, can't use 'em!" This is one item you can live without. Your tongs and spatula will do a much better job without poking holes in your meat. If you have one of these, donate it to your favorite charity.

I highly recommend Der Küchen Laden in Fredericksburg as a source for great kitchen tools: 830-997-4937; www.littlechef.com; https://www.facebook.com/der-kuchenladen. (FULL DISCLOSURE: I liked this store so much that, a few years after finishing this book, I accepted an offer to work there.)

Fire in the Hole!

This section of this book is probably the most important. I believe you can have a piece of meat and a fire and nothing else and produce a tasty barbecue. I do appreciate a little seasoning on my meat, but I want the meat to be the star of this show.

For the meat to have that great barbecue flavor, the fire must be started and maintained properly. Here is how I do it.

Earlier I explained about the East Texas and Central Texas barbecue styles. The barbecue method I have developed lies somewhere in between those two styles and can be used to prepare Texas barbecue easily in one's own backyard.

I use a small Texas-style smoker pit with an offset firebox. The pit is about 4½ feet long and 1½ feet in diameter. I start my fire with natural lump charcoal, using a charcoal chimney, away from the pit on a fireproof surface, to light the coals. I fill the chimney with charcoal and light it with a couple of sheets of newspaper. Once the coals are lit, I put them in the firebox and add half again as much charcoal. I let this burn until all the coals are covered in a thin layer of gray ash. This takes about 30 to 40 minutes total from start to finish.

Here's the "smoke" part: I use small, seasoned hardwood logs. I keep hickory and oak on hand. My first choice is Texas post oak, which produces a medium smoke flavor that is not acrid. I use hickory when I can't get oak. Pecan is good but hard to find. I find the flavor mesquite wood imparts to be too sharp for smoking.

It's important to maintain a relatively consistent temperature in the smoke/meat pit, by regulating the flow of air in and out. Increasing the amount of air flowing into the pit makes the fire burn hotter; decreasing the amount of airflow lowers the temperature. I recommend aiming for a temperature of 250 degrees F in the pit.

When the coals are ready and the temperature is 250 degrees, I place a single small log on top of the coals, close the door on the firebox and put my meat on the pit.

Then I wait. After about an hour, I start another batch of coals using the same method I did with the first batch. When my fire begins to go low after about an hour and a half, I add the coals I have started away from the pit. I try to start a batch of coals every 1 to 1½ hours. If you are using natural charcoal, you can add chunks from the bag directly to the fire if you have to — sometimes it is hard to wake up in the night to go tend the fire — but I prefer to add lit coals, as I believe it reduces the soot level.

If you have a good source for lots of firewood, you can start a fire with logs (instead of charcoal), then wait for the logs to burn down to embers and use those embers for your fire. I do this when I have an abundant supply of firewood. You will need to keep a fire going away from the pit to ensure that embers will be available when you need them, ready to shovel into your firebox. I still put the single small log on top of the embers when I start the cooking. That one log smokes for 3 to 4 hours and provides plenty of smoke without being too strong.

In lieu of the log, you can use chips or chunks of wood you have soaked to produce smoke in your pit, but err on the side of caution lest your meat end up tasting too smoky. I would say the most common mistake barbecue novices make is over-smoking the meat. I struggled for a while to learn this lesson.

The other tricky part that takes practice is keeping the heat consistent. After nine years of using the same pit, my adjustments each time I build a fire are minimal. I had a guest at my house one day when I was cooking a larger amount of barbecue than usual, and each time he passed my pit he glanced at the thermometer. Finally, he asked me if my thermometer was broken, because every time he passed the pit, from early morning to late evening, it read 250 degrees. He didn't realize he was paying me what any pitmaster would consider a supreme compliment!

To Brine or Not to Brine

In brining, you submerge your meat in a solution of salt, water and other seasonings for several hours. Over the last 30-plus years, I have brined all kinds of meat. Brining seems to act as a flavor enhancer and ensure a nice moist barbecue. The difference brining brings to barbecue is nice but subtle; if you don't have enough time to brine, by all means have your barbecue without brining.

You can flavor your brine with aromatics and other seasonings if you like. You won't believe it, but I use a very basic brine.

Basic Brine

You can use this on any meat or fowl; it's enough to brine a good-sized brisket or several pounds of other meat. You'll need a good supply of ice and an ice chest — ideally, one that's just large enough to hold your meat and brine but not a great deal larger, to maximize cooling.

    1 gallon cold water, divided
    1 cup kosher salt
    1 cup sugar

Pour about 3 cups of the water into a saucepan and set over medium-high heat. Stir in the salt and sugar and continue to stir until dissolved.

Add this mixture to the rest of the water, stir to mix and then allow to cool.

Place meat in ice chest. Pour cooled brine over meat. Add enough ice to keep the meat chilled; the temperature should remain below 40 degrees F at all times. Close ice chest securely and leave overnight, or at least 8 hours and up to 24 hours, adding ice when necessary to keep the temperature below 40 degrees.

Remove meat from brine, rinse thoroughly and pat dry.

RECIPES
Rubs, Sauces and Mops

There are many recipes around for sauces, mops, marinades and rubs. Find the ones you like and use them, or create your own. The important issue with barbecue is to do it your way — figure out how to get the taste, texture, flavors and aromas that are appealing to you and your friends and family. There are no rules; don't be afraid to experiment, so you can find "The Way."

In Texas, sauce is something you put on your barbecue after you have cooked it. We like "sauce on the side." There are those folks, however, who believe they must put sauce on their barbecue. If you are one of those people, apply the sauce only during the last few minutes of cooking so the sugars in the sauce won't burn and become bitter.

If you want any of the cooked sauces below to taste smoky, you can put a piece of smoked meat — a ham hock, pork neck or the like — into the sauce mixture while cooking. Introducing meat to your sauce, however, will shorten its shelf life to a few days in the fridge. Remove and discard the meat before using the sauce; if sauce has been refrigerated, bring it to a boil before reusing. If you can stand the heat, a few dried chipotle peppers will add some smoky, spicy flavor.

A mop is a marinade-like mixture, usually including vinegar, applied to the meat while it's cooking. I don't use mops on barbecue. Some folks like to use them, though, so here is a basic mop for basting any meat. For those who feel they must …

To get you started, here are some of the recipes I use.

Wally's Universal Basic Rub

I have been using this rub for 35 years. I use it on any cut of beef, pork and chicken. If you eat barbecue at my house, this is what you will get, most every time.

Thoroughly mix together equal parts salt and freshly ground black pepper. Sprinkle on meat and rub in. If you like it spicier, add a few shakes of ground cayenne pepper.

A note here about black pepper: I think fresh makes a lot of difference. I use an enormous amount of black pepper. It is worth the time to grind fresh.

Pork Rub

This adds flavor to pork ribs. I don't think five-spice powder was invented in Texas, but it tastes good on pork. I have used this on poultry and lamb as well.

Makes about ½ cup

2 tablespoons salt
2 tablespoons freshly ground black pepper
2 tablespoons five-spice powder
1 tablespoon brown sugar
1 tablespoon cayenne pepper
1 teaspoon chili powder

Mix together, sprinkle on meat and rub in.

Everyone Else's Rub

I don't like to use garlic salt, garlic powder, onion powder, etc., in my cooking. Nothing wrong with it, except I don't care for it. I have tried granulated garlic from a company named Spice Hunter, which was OK. Many people use those products and like them, though, and this rub is for all those folks. It also has sugar in it, which I normally don't use in my rubs.

Makes about ½ cup

2 tablespoons brown sugar
2 tablespoons kosher salt
2 tablespoons freshly ground black pepper
2 teaspoons ground cumin
1 teaspoon ancho chili powder
1 teaspoon granulated garlic or garlic powder
1 teaspoon paprika
1 teaspoon cayenne pepper

Mix together and apply liberally to meat.

Wally's Texas Barbecue Sauce

My formula for simple Texas sauce has evolved over many years. I am sure it is not finished yet. I like it thin and peppery. This is a table sauce, good for dippin'. It is always on the table when barbecue is served. Good for a week or so in the fridge; bring to boil before re-using.

- 2 tablespoons olive oil
- 1 medium onion, roughly chopped
- 6 cloves garlic, finely chopped
- 3 tablespoons freshly ground black pepper
- 1 tablespoon cayenne pepper
- 2 teaspoons salt
- 2 teaspoons chili powder
- 1 small cinnamon stick, whole
- 1 clove, whole
- 1 bay leaf, crumbled
- 1 (15-oz.) can tomato sauce
- ⅓ cup beer (you can substitute broth, wine, or water)
- ⅓ cup cider vinegar
- ⅓ cup brown sugar
- ¼ cup strong black coffee

Heat oil in a saucepan over medium heat. Add onion and cook, stirring frequently, until softened (a couple of minutes). Add garlic and sauté for 1 minute.

Stir in pepper, cayenne, salt, chili powder, cinnamon stick, clove and bay leaf; cook, stirring, for 1 minute.

Stir in remaining ingredients, raise heat to high and bring to a boil; then reduce heat to a low simmer. Simmer for 45 minutes to 1 hour, stirring occasionally.

Strain sauce and discard any solids, grind in a bit of black pepper and serve or pour into bottles and refrigerate.

Barbecue Sauce, Ketchup Base

This sauce is simple and uses ingredients most of us have in our kitchens. This one is for ketchup lovers everywhere.

- 1 onion, cut in quarters (no need to peel)
- 4 cloves garlic, smashed (no need to peel)
- ¾ cup ketchup
- ½ cup beer or water
- ¼ cup brown sugar
- 1 tablespoon Worcestershire sauce
- 1 tablespoon freshly ground black pepper
- 2 teaspoons chili powder
- 1½ teaspoon salt
- 1 teaspoon cayenne
- ½ teaspoon dry mustard powder
- 1 bay leaf

Mix all ingredients together in a saucepan. Bring to a boil; then lower heat and simmer, covered, for 45 minutes. Strain, discarding solids, and serve, or store in the fridge for up to 10 days.

No Cookin' Barbecue Sauce

We usually eat barbecue with little or no sauce at home. If you have friends over who whine about not having any sauce, duck into the kitchen and get this made in a minute. Be sure you dissolve the sugar before serving it. We serve it in a clean empty beer bottle (we seem to always have those on hand). You can warm the bottle of sauce in a hot pan of water, if desired.

½ cup ketchup
⅓ cup vinegar
⅓ cup water
3 tablespoons sugar
1 teaspoon salt
1 teaspoon chili powder
½ teaspoon Worcestershire sauce
¼ teaspoon Tabasco or other hot sauce

In a bowl, stir together the ketchup, vinegar and water; add the sugar and seasonings and stir well to make sure the sugar is dissolved. Transfer to a bottle or jar and shake well ... instant sauce!

Coffee Barbecue Sauce

This is a tasty sauce made with strong black coffee. Make sure the coffee is fresh. The sauce keeps for about a week in the fridge.

1 cup ketchup
½ cup strong freshly brewed coffee
¼ cup cider vinegar
1 medium onion, chopped
1 fresh jalapeño, chopped
4 garlic cloves, crushed
½ cup brown sugar
2 tablespoons chili powder
2 tablespoons freshly ground black pepper
1 tablespoon ground cumin
2 teaspoons dry mustard powder
1 teaspoon paprika
½ teaspoon salt

Mix ketchup, coffee and vinegar together in a saucepan; stir in remaining ingredients. Bring to a boil, then reduce to a simmer and cook for 30 to 40 minutes. Strain the sauce, discarding solids, and serve.

LBJ, All the Way

This recipe was given to me a few years ago; it's supposed to be the sauce Lyndon Johnson liked on his ranch in Johnson City. I am not sure this was his recipe, but it is a good sauce to serve on the side with your barbecue.

¼ stick unsalted butter
1 small onion, chopped
2 stalks celery, diced
2 cloves garlic, chopped
1½ cups beer (my preference) or water
¾ cup ketchup
½ cup cider vinegar
3 tablespoons Worcestershire sauce
1 tablespoon sugar
1 tablespoon freshly ground black pepper
1 teaspoon paprika
½ teaspoon salt
2 bay leaves

Melt butter in a saucepan over medium heat; add onion, celery and garlic and cook, stirring, to soften, for a couple of minutes. Stir in remaining ingredients; bring to boil in saucepan, reduce heat and simmer for 30 minutes. Strain, discarding solids, and serve. Keeps 5 to 7 days in the fridge.

Basic Mop

1 cup cider vinegar
1 cup olive oil, bacon fat or your favorite other fat
3 cloves garlic, crushed
2 tablespoons freshly ground black pepper
1 teaspoon salt

Combine all ingredients and use to baste meat while it is cooking.

Beef

Texas Barbecue Brisket

So we come to the Holy Grail of Texas barbecue, the lowly brisket. This inexpensive, tough piece of beef becomes a little bit of barbecue heaven when cooked properly.

Should feed 8 to 10 hungry people with leftovers

I believe there are only three items on the barbecue-brisket ingredient list: a 10-plus-pound brisket, packer trim (the packer cut or trim indicates a whole, minimally trimmed brisket, traditional for Texas barbecue); the rub of your choice (a half-cup or more); and the fire of your choice. That's it!

1. The day before your barbecue, trim any excess fat from your brisket. You want a minimum of a quarter-inch layer of fat. When you get your packer brisket, you will see that you have a lean end and a fat end. The lean end is about 1½ inches thick and the fat end about 4 inches thick. Some folks cut the brisket into two pieces, one thick, one thin, and cook them for different times, to achieve identical doneness. I don't do this.

2. Prepare a brine mixture (page 17) and let your brisket bask in the brine solution overnight.

3. When you're ready to begin barbecuing (at least 12 hours before you're planning to eat the brisket), remove brisket from brine, rinse and pat almost completely dry. I leave a little moisture so the rub will stick.

4. Apply rub liberally. Rub it into the meat. Let the brisket rest while you build a fire and your pit temperature reaches 250 degrees F. Place brisket fat side up in the pit. Place a drip pan under the meat to catch the drippings (which can be used to flavor sauces for the table but will

shorten the shelf life of the sauce). I usually don't worry with a water pan, but if you want, you can add water to the drip pan. That will ensure the drippings won't burn and will introduce some moisture into the pit.

5. Cook the brisket 1 to 1½ hour per pound, maintaining pit temperature at 250. I cook a 10-pound brisket 11 to 12 hours. The long cooking time gives you an opportunity to prepare the other dishes you will be serving, so everything should proceed in a very relaxed, laid-back manner. This is cooking at its best.

6. You should end up with a nice dark bark on the outside of your brisket and a red smoke ring around the inside perimeter. Remove the brisket from the pit and cover loosely with foil. I let my brisket rest at least 30 minutes or more.

7. Cut brisket across the grain and serve. For old hands like me, cut some at a flat angle to get an "in and out" portion.

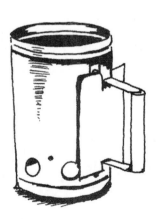

Texas Barbecue Beef Clod

Some people in Texas prefer beef clod — the shoulder, an old-time specialty of Central Texas barbecue joints, especially those in Lockhart — to brisket. The meat is a little leaner than brisket but still has plenty of flavor. A whole beef clod can weigh over 20 pounds, a large size to cook on a home pit. If you like clod, have your butcher cut a 3- to 5-pound roast for you; it will serve four to six people and should cook in a few hours.

Should feed 4 to 6 with leftovers

Again, you'll need only a 3- to 5-pound beef shoulder clod roast and the rub of your choice (¼ cup or more).

1. You can choose to brine or not. If you do, after brining overnight (see page 17), remove meat from brine, rinse and pat it to remove excess moisture, leaving meat damp so the rub will stick.

2. Apply rub liberally. Rub it into the meat. Let the coated meat rest while you build a fire and bring it to between 250 and 275 degrees F. Place meat on pit with a drip pan underneath to catch drippings. If you have a roast that is light on fat, you will want to add a little water to your drip pan at the beginning of your cooking to introduce some moisture into the pit.

3. Cook for 1 hour per pound. You can turn it halfway through the cooking process.

4. You should end up with a nice bark on the outside and a red smoke ring around the inside perimeter. Remove from pit and cover loosely with foil. Allow to rest for at least 20 minutes.

5. Cut across the grain and serve.   The meat should be tender but not falling apart.

Texts Barbecue Enchiladas

I created these one day while I was trying to find a creative use for leftover brisket. Very tasty!

Should feed 4 to 6

6 to 8 cups chicken broth (preferably homemade)
1 dried chipotle pepper (use more if you want the sauce very spicy hot)
1⅓ cup fat of your choice — olive oil, bacon fat, lard, etc. — **divided**
1 cup flour
1 clove garlic, minced
1 tablespoon Gebhardt's Chili Powder
½ teaspoon cumin powder
½ teaspoon smoked paprika
Pinch curry powder (if you can easily taste the curry powder in the sauce, you've put in too much)
1½ teaspoons salt
12 corn tortillas
1½ to 2 cups chopped cooked Barbecue Brisket (see page 28)
1 pound medium Cheddar cheese, grated
1 large onion, chopped

In a large saucepan over high heat, bring chicken broth to a broil and immediately reduce heat to maintain a low simmer. (While the broth is heating, you can chop the brisket and onions and grate the cheese.)

Pour a little of the hot broth into a small bowl and add chipotle pepper; set aside to soak for about 20 minutes.

Pre-heat oven to 350 degrees F.

To make the sauce, heat 1 cup of the oil or fat in a 3- to 4-quart sauté pan or Dutch oven over medium heat. Add the flour and stir to make a light roux. Cook, stirring, for a couple of minutes to remove the raw flour taste, but do not brown.

Stir garlic into the roux; then stir in chili powder, cumin, paprika and curry powder; blend thoroughly.

Gradually whisk chicken broth into the roux, whisking until any lumps are eliminated. Add reconstituted chipotle pepper and salt. Stir, bring mixture to a low simmer and adjust heat to maintain a low simmer for 20 minutes; then remove pan from heat.

Ladle a thin layer of the sauce into the bottom of a baking dish, lasagna pan, casserole or other dish large enough to hold 12 enchiladas without crowding; set the saucepan of sauce near the stove so you can dip the hot tortillas in it as they removed from the hot oil as instructed below.

In an 8- or 9-inch skillet, heat the remaining ⅓ cup oil or fat over medium-high heat. Test the temperature by dipping an edge of tortilla in the oil: It should bubble and sizzle. Using tongs or a wooden spatula, dip a tortilla in the oil on both sides, just for a couple of seconds a side. You are trying to "seal" and soften the tortilla. (I use my fingers to do this, very carefully dipping the tortilla almost all the way into the oil. This technique was handed down to me from my mother. For safety reasons, I don't recommend you try it, but it is interesting to watch.) Hold the tortilla over the hot oil to drain for a few seconds; then blot it on a clean towel or paper towel. Immediately dip the tortilla into the sauce mixture to coat both sides. (Here again I use my fingers, but tongs will work fine too.)

Place the tortilla on a work surface. Spread 2 or 3 tablespoons of the chopped brisket down the center of the tortilla; top with an equal amount of shredded cheese and a sprinkling of onion (you will need to apportion so that all the brisket is used inside the enchiladas but some of the cheese and onion are left to sprinkle atop the finished enchiladas). Fold one side of tortilla over filling, tuck it tightly back under the filling, roll the enchilada up neatly and tightly and place in baking dish. Repeat with remaining tortillas, leaving a little room between each enchilada.

When all enchiladas are neatly arranged in baking dish, cover them completely with a blanket of sauce. Sprinkle remaining onion and cheese on top. Cover with foil and bake in pre-heated 350-degree oven for 20 to 25 minutes. Remove foil and bake 5 to 10 minutes more, until topping is bubbling.

Remove pan from oven, cover loosely with foil and allow to rest for 5 to 10 minutes before serving.

Serve rice and beans on the side and plenty of cold beverages. For an extra kick, pass a bowl of Chile Macho (see recipe below).

Chile Macho

We always top our enchiladas with this fresh salsa. The recipe has been handed down in my family. My father puts it on everything.

When you select your jalapeños at the market, look for ones with a smooth skin, a nice dark-green color and little light-colored lines running the length of the pepper. The lines are an indication of ripeness.

Note to non-Texans: OK, this can be very hot. There are those folks who add a tomatillo or two, or even a tomato or two. Removing the seeds and stems from the peppers takes away much of the heat. I wouldn't, but there are those who do.

12 ripe jalapeños
12 cloves garlic
Dash of salt
Juice of 1 lemon or lime
Scant few drops of vinegar

Remove stems from jalapeños and coarsely chop.

Smash garlic with blade of a heavy knife and remove peel.

Place jalapeños and garlic in food processor. Using brief pulses of the processor, chop mixture completely and evenly. Transfer mixture to a container; add salt, lemon juice and vinegar, stirring until thoroughly mixed in. Let the mixture sit for at least a couple of hours.

Texas Barbecue Beef Top Sirloin

Should feed 4 to 6 hungry people

2½ to 3½ pounds beef top sirloin, cut 2 to 2½ inches thick
1 teaspoon olive oil
¼ cup rub of choice; I use just salt and freshly ground black pepper

Remove sirloin from fridge at least 30 minutes before it will go on the pit. Rub it all over with oil. Apply rub liberally, rubbing it into the meat. Let meat rest while you build a fire with your favorite wood; I use pecan or oak for this. Be sure you have a little smoke, but it doesn't take much. Maintain the temperature at 330 to 350 degrees F. Place a water-filled pan underneath meat to catch drippings and provide a little moisture.

Close pit and cook for 15 to 20 minutes per pound, turning beef half-way through cooking. I like to cook it to the rare side of medium, taking it off when the beef's internal temperature reaches about 130 degrees F (the temperature will continue to rise a bit as the meat rests).

Remove meat from pit and cover *loosely* with foil. Allow to rest for at least 20 minutes.

Slice across the grain and serve.

Steak in the Coals

Sometimes, when I start my fire to barbecue, I don't want to wait for hours to chow down on some great Texas beef. So, when the coals become gray embers, I opt for a ribeye or New York strip steak.

Burt Finger from Photographs Do Not Bend Gallery in Dallas told me about this method of cooking steak a number of years ago, but it took me a couple of years to get around to trying it. I have not tried it with wood embers, only charcoal.

Alton Brown on the Food Network cooked a steak in this manner on his show a few years ago, and he used a hair dryer to blow the ash off the coals before putting the steak on. Could be a valid idea if you have a problem with ashes on your steak. I never seem to have a hair dryer near my barbecue pit. The fact that I am hair-challenged might have something to do with that.

Look for a steak at least 1½ inches thick; closer to 2 inches is even better. Apply some kosher salt and place your steak directly on the coals. Close the pit and let the steak cook, with air damper closed, for 5 minutes. Turn steak over and cook for 4 minutes. You will have a slightly crusty, charred exterior with a rare center. Delicious!

Barbacoa

My father grew up in and around Mason, Texas. He had to quit school after the second grade to help his family pick crops like cotton and onions. By the time he was a teenager, he knew how to do just about everything. His father taught him how to make barbacoa the same way his grandfather had taught his father.

This is what my father told me, greatly simplified: Dig a hole; build a fire; add a goat, lamb, cow's head or pig that has been seasoned with salt, pepper, chiles, onions, garlic, etc., and wrapped in wet tow sacks. Cover with more wet tow sacks or banana leaves. Fill the pit with dirt, build another fire on top of the pit; then wait 12 hours, uncover, and have barbacoa.

I have modified this procedure to make it a little more user-friendly and keep the dirt and sand out of the barbecue:

1. Dig a pit about 1 foot bigger in each direction than the animal you are going to cook. Make the pit 2 to 3 feet deep. Line the bottom and side of the pit with bricks. Find a piece of metal, such as tin, to cover the pit.

2. Build a fire in the pit with lots of wood. When that fire burns down some, add more wood. You want to end up with about 12 inches of embers. Depending on how big your pit is, this could take 8 hours or more.

3. Prepare your meat for the fire by using your favorite rub or seasonings. Wrap the meat with any combination of banana leaves, wet burlap sacks, wet cheesecloth or such. Wrap the whole bundle in a couple of layers of chicken wire to facilitate removal from the pit and to keep the meat from making direct contact with the embers.

4. Put the tin cover over the pit and shovel the dirt that came out of the hole over the tin, to cover completely. Go play some horseshoes, have a few beers, take a siesta, wake up and take a shower, have a few more beers, make some coffee, have a snack, and be patient. In about 11 or 12 hours you can eat.

5. Remove the dirt, the cover and the meat. Serve immediately with fiery hot salsa, cilantro and onions on hot tortillas. *Qué lástima!* What a shame I am not there right now!

Note: You can cook beans, other vegetables, soups, stews and sauces in the pit with your meat. In some parts of Mexico they put pots of broth under the meat to catch the drippings. The broth is considered to be a real treat.

Beef Ribs

We always think of Texas barbecue as beef, yet you rarely see beef ribs served in barbecue Joints. Odd, isn't it?

I love beefy barbecue ribs. You can sometimes find beef back ribs in your meat counter; if not, ask your butcher to order some for you. Alternatively, you could buy a whole rib section, cut off the ribs for barbecue, cut out a roast (which you can barbecue!) and have some rib-eye steaks left over for grilling.

I used to buy a whole prime rib section the day before Thanksgiving. I would ask my butcher to hang it in his cooler until Christmas Eve. This dry aging caused the meat to shrink by about 15 percent to 20 percent, which made it very expensive per pound but gave it an intense beef flavor that was incredible. The texture was dense and almost silky. It was the color of dark red wine. I would roast the eye of rib for Christmas Dinner, prepare some great rib-eye steaks after Christmas and save the ribs for a really special barbecue.

Here is how to fix some tasty ribs on your pit.

1. Buy one or two racks of beef ribs with a good layer of fat.
2. Remove the membrane from the back of the ribs using a dull knife, such as a butter knife, or a Phillips screwdriver, and paper towels for grip. Once you get a corner of the membrane pulled up, you grab it with a paper towel and pull it off. The idea is to pull the membrane away from the ribs without cutting or tearing the membrane so that it comes off in one piece.
3. I rub my beef ribs with a little olive oil, then dry slightly with a paper towel. For the rub, I use lots of freshly ground black pepper and salt, but I don't like the rub to be thick. Use your favorite rub on the ribs and let them rest while you start your fire.
4. When pit temperature is 250 degrees F, add a very small amount of wood for smoke and place ribs on the pit membrane side up. Cook for 1½ hours; then turn. Cook for another 3 to 4 hours, maybe 4½ hours

more if you are cooking two racks. You should see the meat begin to shrink and pull away from the bones. Do not overcook. The meat should be easy to bite off the bone but should not "fall off."

5. If you like your ribs wet, apply your choice of sauce during last 45 minutes to 1 hour of cooking to allow ribs to glaze.

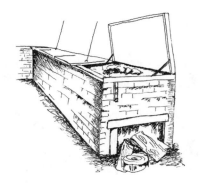

Pork

Barbecue Ham

When I was a boy, my family used to get ham, sausage and brisket from John's Barbecue in Houston. We would buy enough to enjoy our barbecue for a couple of days. The ham was just right, with a good, salty, smoky flavor. Most barbecue joints nowadays don't serve ham, and that is too bad. My recipe is an attempt to replicate that ham at John's barbecue, on Crockett Street in Houston, circa 1960.

Should feed 12 to 16

1 pre-cooked smoked ham (I buy shanks, about 8 to 10 pounds)

Because the shanks are cured and cooked, the only treatment I give them is to coat them well with freshly ground black pepper.

Build fire to maintain 275 degree F pit temperature.

Place ham in pit face-down. These hams have lots of moisture in them, but if you are worried about dryness, use a water pan in your smoker for at least half the cooking time.

You will cook the ham for 15 minutes per pound. You are looking for an internal temperature of 160 degrees F. When that temperature is reached, remove ham from smoker and cover loosely with foil to rest for 30 minutes; then slice and serve.

Be sure to save the ham bone for soup or, better yet, a pot of beans. The ham bones were always treasured and highly sought after in my old neighborhood.

Barbecue Pork Shoulder

Even though beef is supreme in Texas, we will cook a pork butt now and then for some of our friends who escaped to Texas from parts of the South. This is easy and tasty.

Should feed 8 to 10

2 tablespoons salt
2 tablespoons freshly ground black pepper
1 tablespoon paprika
1 teaspoon cayenne
½ teaspoon five-spice powder
1 pork roast from shoulder (butt roast), about 5 pounds

Blend all ingredients but pork together to make rub. Apply rub to roast up to 24 hours before cooking. I usually apply a few hours before.

Prepare your fire to cook at 250 to 275 degrees F. I use oak or hickory. Add some water to your drip tray at the beginning of the cooking process.

Place roast on grill. Cook 4½ to 5 hours, turning halfway through, to an internal temperature of about 170 degrees F.

Remove roast from grill, cover loosely with foil and let rest 20 minutes before serving. I slice it ½-inch thick. Your Southern friends may want to "pull" the pork. Humor them and let them do it.

Texas Barbecue Double-Thick Pork Chops

Should feed 4 hungry people

4 double-thick pork loin chops, at least 2 inches thick
1 teaspoon olive oil
¼ cup rub of your choice (I like to use just salt and freshly ground black pepper)

Remove chops from fridge at least 30 minutes before they will go on the pit. Rub chops all over with oil. Apply rub liberally; rub it into the meat.

Let the chops rest while you build a fire with your favorite wood. I use oak for this. Make sure you get a little smoke, but not too much. Maintain the temperature at 350-375 degrees F. Put water in a pan under meat to catch drippings and provide a little moisture.

Cook for about 20 to 25 minutes per pound. Turn chops halfway through cooking. I take them off at 155 degrees F internal temperature.

Remove from pit and cover loosely with foil. Allow to rest for at least 10 minutes before serving.

Barbecue Pig

You'll need to order a dressed suckling pig from your butcher in advance.

Should feed 6 to 8

1 suckling pig, 10 to 15 pounds, dressed
½ cup olive oil
½ cup rub of choice
1 small apple

Remove pig from fridge and let come to room temperature.

Rub pig all over with oil and apply rub liberally (or just use salt and pepper).

Build a fire of your choice. I use pecan with a dab of hickory for smoke. Maintain your fire at 325 to 350 degrees F.

Place pig in pit with butt toward fire.

When the snout, ears and tail start to turn brown, cover them with heavy-duty aluminum foil.

Cook to an internal temperature of 155 degrees F, about 20 minutes per pound.

Remove pig from pit, cover loosely with foil and let rest for 10 to 15 minutes before carving and serving.

Barbecue Pork Steaks

In the '90s, every time I drove anywhere near Hallettsville, I made a bee-line to Novosad's barbecue. These folks did a good job with the usual brisket, sausage and ribs, but they also did really fine lamb ribs and pork steaks. I love both of those. Here is my version of barbecue pork steaks.

Should feed 6

3 pounds pork steaks cut from pork butt (have your butcher cut these about ¾-inch thick with his saw)

⅓ cup rub of your choice (I use freshly ground black pepper, salt, a little cayenne and a little annatto powder)

Remove steaks from refrigerator 30 minutes before cooking. Apply rub to steaks and let sit for 20 to 30 minutes.

Prepare fire and adjust for 275 degrees F. I use oak.

Place steaks in pit. You will probably want some water in your drip pan. Cook for about 3 to 3½ hours. Internal temp should be 170 degrees F.

Remove from grill, cover loosely and let rest for 10 to 15 minutes before serving.

Barbecue Spareribs

Even though beef is king in Texas, when we talk about barbecue ribs, we usually mean pork ribs. They are juicy and delicious, not too expensive, easy to find, and nothing could be easier to prepare. I buy the rack and trim the flap and cartilage tips, or you can buy St.-Louis-style ribs, which are already trimmed and easier for most folks to deal with.

A rack should serve 2 to 4

1. Take the membrane off the back of the ribs by using a dull knife, like a butter knife, and paper towels for grip. Once you get a corner of the membrane pulled up you grab it with a paper towel and pull it off.
2. Apply your favorite rub. I don't like the rub to be thick; a little goes a long way.
3. While the meat rests, prepare your fire and regulate temperature to 250 degrees F. Add a small log or a few chunks of wood for a nice smoky flavor.
4. Place the ribs membrane side up in the pit. You will want to turn the ribs after about 1 to 1½ hours. Total cooking time for one rack is about 4½ to 5 hours; two racks takes about another half-hour. You want to bite the meat away from the bone, not have it slide off.
5. If you are of the "wet ribs" crowd, baste the ribs with your favorite sauce during the last hour of cooking so they will develop a glaze.

Wally's Texas Sausage

You'll need a meat grinder and sausage stuffer to make traditional sausage with casings. If you have a KitchenAid mixer, you can purchase both meat-grinding and sausage-stuffing attachments for it. Sausage-making tools and equipment are also available at specialty kitchen stores and online, you can buy casings at butcher shops and online.

You can also make sausage without a dedicated meat grinder, sausage stuffer or casings — just follow the instructions in the note at the end of the recipe.

Keeping your meat and your sausage-making equipment cool is helpful to keep the fat from melting. You can place your grinder and sausage stuffer in the freezer for about 15 minutes before using. And you can work with a small amount of meat mixture at a time while stuffing, keeping the rest in the fridge.

Should feed 8 to 10

2 pounds pork shoulder with fat
1 pound beef chuck with fat
1 small onion, minced
6 cloves garlic, minced
1 tablespoon freshly ground black pepper
1 tablespoon crushed red pepper
2 teaspoons salt
1½ teaspoons ground sage
½ teaspoon cayenne
Sausage casings
Olive oil, lard or bacon fat for brushing

With a meat grinder, grind the meats coarsely.

Place ground meat in a large bowl and mix in onion, garlic and seasonings, making sure all ingredients are evenly distributed. Refrigerate for at least two hours, up to overnight.

Soak the casings in warm water for 30 minutes and drain. Flush by running warm water through each in your sink.

Set up the sausage stuffer. Take one casing and slip it onto the extrusion tube, leaving about 6 inches at the end, untied. Pack the meat mixture into the body of the sausage stuffer. Crank very slowly until you see the meat emerging from the tube. Using kitchen twine, tie a knot at the end of the casing and gradually crank the sausage into the casing. Watch carefully and do not overstuff; when the casing reaches 1¼ inches thick and about 5 inches long, tie it off with kitchen twine and continue stuffing with remaining casing.

Refrigerate sausages until ready to smoke, overnight if necessary.

Prepare a fire for cooking at 250 degrees F.

Brush sausages *lightly* with oil or fat. Place in pit and cook for 2 hours.

NOTE: OK, so let's say you don't have sausage casings or a meat grinder. You can use a food processor to grind the meats with the garlic and onion. The secret here is to use only pulse to grind; *do not over-process.* Pulse until all meat is ground and garlic, onion and seasonings are well mixed.

To make sausages without casing, form the ground meat mixture into balls, then roll the balls between your hands to get a sausage shape about 1½ inches in diameter and 4 to 5 inches long.

Refrigerate until ready to cook; then smoke as described above.

Lamb and Goat

Barbecue Leg of Lamb

I love lamb. Lamb chops, lamb stew, lamb shanks, leg of lamb, lamb spare-ribs — Bob's Smokehouse near the Alamodome in San Antonio used to serve great lamb spareribs; it's now the Old Smokehouse, but lamb ribs are still on the menu. I fix a Texas lamb leg on my smoker that is simple and delicious.

I use a very simple rub for this, just salt and freshly ground black pepper. James Beard used to roast lamb with just salt and pepper, and he was a pretty smart cook. He was not from Texas — rather, Oregon — but he must have lived in Texas in a previous life. He understood and appreciated good barbecue.

Should feed 8 to 12

3 tablespoons salt
3 tablespoons freshly ground black pepper
1 leg of lamb, bone in, about 6 pounds

Mix salt and pepper together to make rub.

About a half-hour before cooking, remove lamb from fridge and apply rub liberally all over, rubbing it into surface of meat.

Prepare fire to cook at 325 degrees F. You want only a little smoke as not to overpower the lamb flavor.

Place lamb in pit and cook, fat side up, for about 3 to 3½ hours. Be sure you do not overcook. For medium-rare, the internal temperature should be 130 to 135 degrees F when you remove from the grill; for medium rare, 140 to 145 degrees.

Cover loosely and let rest for 15 to 20 minutes before slicing into ½-inch thick slices to serve.

Barbecue Cabrito

We have been eating goat in Texas for hundreds of years. There is a wonderful barbecue goat cook-off in Brady every Labor Day weekend. If you don't love barbecue goat before you go there, you will by the time you leave.

This recipe produces a really tasty barbecued cabrito — kid, or young goat. I serve it with frijoles a la charra (recipe, page 55), fresh chiles, hot tortillas and cold beer.

Should feed 8 to 12

1. You'll want to order an 8- to 10-pound kid from your butcher in advance (if your regular butcher doesn't handle kid, try a Hispanic *carniceria* or meat market). Specify that the kid be dressed and butterflied to lay flat on the grill.

2. You will want to brine the goat before cooking, as it can get dry in the cooking process. I use some water in my drip pan as well to keep it moist.

3. I make a moist rub of ½ cup olive oil; 3 tablespoons vinegar; 2 tablespoons lemon or lime juice; 2 to 3 cloves of garlic, minced; 3 tablespoons salt; 2 tablespoons freshly ground black pepper; 1 or 2 bay leaves, crushed; ½ teaspoon ground cayenne; and a small bunch of cilantro, roughly chopped. You want the consistency to be between a sauce and a paste. Rub thoroughly all over the cabrito.

4. like post oak as my choice of wood for cabrito. The temperature should be 275 degrees F. When the fire is ready, place goat in pit. Cook for 3 to 4 hours at 275 to 300 degrees F, turning halfway through. Do not overcook; internal temp should be 140 to 145 degrees F.

5. Remove from pit and let rest for 15 to 20 minutes.

Fowl

One-Arm Chicken

I try to be very consistent when barbecuing, but I will now be inconsistent. I have mentioned previously that I do not like to marinate meat for barbecue … BUT I do use a marinade for barbecue chicken. I also use a rub, which I make with salt, freshly ground black pepper, paprika and a little bit of cayenne.

I was doing a series of cooking demos in California in the '80s and had a regular heckler in the audience. I think he came to the daily demos just to heckle me. I was cutting up a chicken when he distracted me with a goofy comment. As I looked up to retort, I cut a finger on my left hand, pretty deeply. This, of course, excited everyone, and my heckler was freaked out and very remorseful. As it turned out, he was trained in first aid and had a real first-aid kit in his car. He retrieved the kit and sutured my cut with a "butterfly" and a large amount of gauze and tape. I continued the demo, using only my right hand, keeping my left hand elevated as Dr. Heckle advised. I named the recipe "One-Arm Chicken." This isn't exactly the same recipe, but I like the name.

Should feed 2 to 4

1 fryer, about 3 pounds, cleaned and butterflied
½ cup olive oil
½ cup vinegar
3 cloves garlic, minced
Salt and freshly ground pepper to taste
¼ cup rub of your choice

Brine chicken overnight as directed on page 17.
Make marinade: Mix olive oil, vinegar, garlic, salt and pepper together and set aside.

Remove bird from brine; rinse and dry. Place in large zip-close plastic storage bag and add marinade. Refrigerate to marinate for 1 to 2 hours.

Remove bird from bag and pat dry. Apply rub of your choice.

Place bird in prepared pit, bone side down, and cook at 275 to 300 F. You will want plenty of smoke.

Cook for 1½ hours until internal temp is 160 F.

Remove from pit. Tent loosely with foil.

Let rest for 15 minutes before serving.

Barbecue Quail

I usually grill quail, because they cook fast and I just cannot wait to eat them! Here is a smoked version for when you have the time and patience to wait. If you bird-hunt, or have a generous friend who does, count your blessings to be able to get wild quail; otherwise, find the plumper but blander farm-raised birds at butcher shops and larger or specialty supermarkets.

Should feed 2 to 4, depending on size of quail and appetites

8 quail, cleaned and dressed
¼ cup rub of choice
8 strips of bacon

Start fire.

Wash and dry the quail. Apply the rub of your choice, rubbing all over quail.

Wrap each bird with a strip of bacon, using a toothpick or twine to secure.

When pit temperature is between 250 and 275 degrees F, place quail in pit and close lid. Cook 1 to 1½ hours. Juices should run clear when done.

Smoked Turkey

My family loves smoked turkey, and I like cooking these birds. Try to find a smaller bird, about 12 pounds. Turkeys take well to brining, but it's not essential.

Should feed 8 to 12

12-pound turkey, rinsed and dried
¼ cup salt
¼ cup freshly ground black pepper
¼ teaspoon cayenne pepper
½ cup olive oil or melted butter

If brining, follow instructions on page 17 and let turkey brine overnight.

Make rub by mixing together salt, black pepper and cayenne.

Remove turkey from brine; rinse inside and out and pat both exterior and interior dry thoroughly with paper towels. Rub bird with oil, coating all surfaces inside and out. Apply rub generously inside and out.

Prepare fire to cook at 275 to 300 degrees F. Do not add too much wood; a little smoke goes a long way with turkey. Pour some water into your drip pan.

Place bird in pit, breast side down, with drip pan below, and cook for 2 hours. Turn bird so breast side is up and cook 2 hours.

When internal temperature of bird reaches 160 to 165 degrees F, remove turkey from pit, loosely cover and let rest at least 20 minutes before carving and serving.

Other Beasts

Barbecue Shark

When I was about 12 years old, I came home one Saturday afternoon to see a steady stream of smoke coming from my mom's barbecue pit. I did some chores and took a shower. When I went into the kitchen, I saw what I thought was a big chunk of smoked beef sitting on the table. My mom's back was turned to me, so I felt safe sneaking a piece of meat. Without turning around, my mom asked, "How did you like it?" I was caught! (She had eyes in the back of her head.) I told her it was good but had a different texture from what I was expecting. She told me it was shark. My dad had caught a very large shark that morning and brought it home to see if Mom could cook it.

The shark was really good. The meat looked like a beef shoulder chunk; it was briny and tasty, with just enough smoke.

My mom and Julia Child were the smartest cooks I ever met. I learned a lot from both of them. My mom was from Texas; Julia Child was from California, but she loved Texas barbecue. I saw her do a cooking show where she was having a barbecue, dressed in cowgirl gear and wearing a ten-gallon hat!

I don't really have a recipe for barbecue shark, but I will create one if I ever get the opportunity.

Sides

Frijoles a la Charra

These beans are a nice addition to any barbecue, especially when the weather starts to get a little chilly. Some call 'em beans; others call it soup. Take your pick. They have a little heat and terrific aroma.

I used to teach some cooking classes years ago in California. One class that was always full was "Tex-Mex 101." This recipe came from that class. Once, the Princess and I were invited to a party miles away from our neighborhood in Huntington Beach. Everyone was to bring a dish to share at the party, and we brought some finger foods. When I walked in the kitchen, there was a big pot of frijoles on the stove. I looked in the pot, inhaled the aroma and grabbed a spoon to taste. These seemed to be as good as mine or maybe even better! I asked the hostess who brought the beans and she pointed out a woman in the crowd. I approached her and asked what she put in the beans. Her reply was "You should know. I got the recipe at your cooking class." We must have served many margaritas at that class ... I sure didn't remember her.

Should feed 10 to 12; leftover frijoles are even better the next day

1 pound (2 cups) pinto beans, washed and picked through to remove any stones or wizened beans

2 tablespoons canola oil or olive oil

1 medium onion, chopped

6 cloves garlic, sliced thin

1 small bunch fresh epazote (see note), tied with string for easy retrieval.

1 tablespoon freshly ground black pepper

2 teaspoons dried Mexican oregano

2 teaspoons chili powder

2 teaspoons ground cumin
4 dried bay leaves
1 or 2 good-sized smoked ham hocks
4 medium tomatoes, peeled, seeded and chopped
12-oz. bottle or can of beer
1 bell pepper, chopped
1 jalapeño, sliced
1 Anaheim chile, sliced
1 banana pepper (I use hot ones), chopped
2 tablespoons salt
1 teaspoon sugar
½ cup chopped green onions
½ cup coarsely chopped cilantro leaves

Wash pinto beans and sort through to remove any stones or wizened beans. In a 4- to 6-quart pot, soak beans in water to cover overnight. When ready to cook, drain beans in a colander and return to pot. Refill the pot with cold water, covering the beans by 2 to 3 inches. Bring to a boil; then reduce to a medium simmer. Cover with a lid left slightly askew.

Meanwhile, heat oil in skillet over medium heat and add onion; sauté a few minutes. Add garlic and sauté a couple of minutes, just until soft. Do not burn.

Add epazote, black pepper, Mexican oregano, chili powder, cumin and bay leaves to skillet; cook, stirring, for a minute or two, but don't burn the spices.

Stir mixture in skillet into beans in pot; add ham hock(s). Place slightly tilted cover back on pot, return beans to a medium simmer and cook for an hour and 15 minutes, skimming off any foamy scum as necessary.

Add tomatoes, beer, bell and hot peppers, salt (don't add it any earlier; it could toughen the beans) and sugar. Stir to mix and cook, with lid slightly askew, for another hour and 15 minutes. Check beans for tenderness; if not soft, continue cooking another half-hour or until soft. Taste and add more black pepper and additional salt, if necessary.

Top with green onions and cilantro; serve with Texas barbecue and hot tortillas.

Muy sabroso!

NOTE: Epazote is a traditional Mexican cooking herb used especially in beans. Better go to your local Mexican market for this. Alas, there is no substitute, so leave it out if you must.

Barbecue Beans

I confess I am not a big fan of barbecue beans. Most are too sweet and gloppy. When pressed, I will fix a version of them I find palatable. White beans are traditional for barbecue beans, but you can use other types of beans if you like. Cook them slowly.

Should feed 10 to 12

1 pound (2 cups) dried beans
1 piece smoked ham, about 4 ounces, diced
1 onion, diced
3 cloves garlic, sliced thin
½ teaspoon salt
½ teaspoon freshly ground black pepper
¼ teaspoon cayenne pepper
¾ cup barbecue sauce of your choice
¼ cup apple cider vinegar
1 tablespoon molasses
½ cup beer
½ cup water

Soak beans overnight in water to cover in a large saucepan or pot. Drain; return beans to pot and add smoked ham and fresh water to cover by 1½ to 2 inches. Cover, bring to a boil and reduce heat to maintain a simmer; recover and cook for about 1½ hours, just until skins of beans begin to break.

Preheat oven to 300 degrees F. Drain beans and transfer to a large baking dish. Stir in onions, garlic, salt, pepper and cayenne.

In a separate bowl, mix together barbecue sauce, vinegar and molasses; add beer and water; blend well. Pour this mixture evenly over the beans.

Cover with foil and cook for 4 hours. Remove from oven and let rest 10 minutes before removing foil and serving.

Black-Eyed Peas

Should feed 10 to 12

1 pound (2 cups) dried black-eyed peas
1 teaspoon olive oil
3 slices bacon, diced
1 small onion, diced
2 cloves garlic, sliced
2 teaspoon fresh ground black pepper
2 teaspoons salt

Leaves from small bunch fresh cilantro, chopped

Soak peas overnight in fresh tap water to cover; drain and rinse peas in a colander.

Heat oil in a Dutch oven over medium heat. Add bacon. Cook for 1 to 2 minutes to render fat.

Add onion and cook for 3 to 5 minutes, stirring to cook evenly; do not brown. Add garlic and cook for 2 to 3 minutes without browning.

Add drained and rinsed peas, stir and cover with fresh water, 2 inches over depth of beans. Add black pepper. Cover Dutch oven, leaving lid slightly askew; bring to a boil, reduce to a simmer and cook for 2 hours, stirring in salt toward end of cooking.

When beans are tender, remove from heat, taste for seasoning and add more salt and/or pepper if necessary. Add cilantro, stir and serve. Pass hot sauce on the side.

Lima Beans

Should feed 10 to 12

1 pound (2 cups) dried lima beans
1 large onion, diced
3 cloves garlic, sliced
1 ham hock
1 teaspoon freshly ground black pepper
Pinch of sugar
1 tablespoon salt

Soak beans overnight in a large pot in fresh tap water to cover.
Drain through a colander; return beans to pot and cover with fresh water by 2 to 3 inches. Add onion, garlic, ham hock, pepper and sugar. Cover, bring to a high simmer and then reduce heat to a medium simmer. Cook for 3 to 4 hours, until soft and creamy; stir in salt toward end of cooking. Taste for seasoning before serving. Pass hot sauce on the side.

Wally's Trifecta Coleslaw

John's Barbecue, on Crockett Street in Houston, was my standard for barbecue when I was growing up on Houston's Near North Side. Everything was just sublime. The coleslaw there was bare-bones delicious, very simple, tangy and crisp. I never had coleslaw like that anywhere else other than my house. I was never able to get John's recipe, but this has the same flavor profile my taste buds remember. I added the collard greens, just because I like them so much.

Should feed 8 to 10

¼ cup olive oil
⅓ cup apple cider vinegar
1 to 2 tablespoons freshly ground black pepper
1 teaspoon Dijon mustard
½ to 1 teaspoon salt, to taste
½ teaspoon sugar
3 cups green cabbage, shredded
3 cups red cabbage, shredded
3 cups collard greens, shredded

Mix all ingredients except greens in a large bowl, whisking to blend. Add greens, toss, taste and adjust seasoning if necessary. Should be crisp, tart and peppery.

Collard Greens

*I use collards because I love them, but you can use any green you like —
mustard, turnip or others. I particularly like collards' texture. You can add a
pork neck, salt pork or ham bone if you like. I like 'em plain and simple. The
pot liquor is tart and tasty. You can add more vinegar if you want them to
jump out of the pot!*

Should feed 6 to 10

2 bunches collard greens
½ cup cider vinegar
3 tablespoons salt
½ teaspoon sugar

While bringing about 1½ gallons of water to a boil in a large covered
pot, thoroughly wash collards to remove all grit. Cut out and discard
tough stems and chop leaves into bite-sized pieces.

Add vinegar, salt, sugar and greens to boiling water, return to a boil
and reduce heat to medium-low. Cover and cook greens for about 1 to
1½ hours. Adjust the salt to your taste.

Pass hot sauce or hot-pepper vinegar on the side.

Barbecue Corn

This is a great side to serve with barbecue. It will provide a great corn flavor with smoky overtones.

I have brined the corn before cooking (see page 17) and also prepared it without brining, and brining seems to make the corn a little sweeter and moister. If you don't brine, give the unshucked ears a quick soak in some salty water before cooking. Rinse them and pat them dry before cooking, but don't shuck them. It is very important to cook the corn in the shuck with silk and all. This helps impart the sweet, roasted flavor. The silk comes off very easily with the shucks after cooking.

If you are barbecuing something like quail that doesn't take hours to cook, you can place the ears in your pit with the meat when you start cooking. Temperature should be 350 degrees F. It will take about 40 minutes to cook 4 large ears of corn. Remove from pit and keep warm until time to serve.

If, however, the meat is something that takes hours to cook, put the corn on the pit for 15 minutes to absorb the smoky flavor, then remove, cover loosely and put aside until about 30 minutes before the meat is ready to come off the pit; then place corn in a pre-heated 350 degree F oven for 30 minutes to finish cooking before serving with your barbecue.

I have also roasted corn like this in a 350-degree oven for 35 to 40 minutes without putting it on the pit first, and it results in deep corn flavor. This is my method of choice these days.

German Potato Salad

Because the German settlers in Texas had such a huge influence on the evolution of Texas barbecue, I include this potato salad recipe made in the German style. This salad is to be served warm.

Should feed 6 to 8

6 medium potatoes, peeled (if using red potatoes, use 8)
3 teaspoons salt, divided
⅓ cup apple cider vinegar
3 teaspoons sugar
8 slices bacon
1 small onion, diced fine
4 tablespoons chopped parsley
Freshly ground black pepper to taste

In a large pot, cover the potatoes with water and add 1½ teaspoons of the salt. Bring to a boil, reduce to a medium simmer and cook until barely fork-tender. Drain potatoes and cut into bite-sized pieces.

While potatoes are cooking, whisk together vinegar, sugar and remaining 1½ teaspoons salt in a small bowl and set aside.

In a skillet, fry the bacon until crisp; remove bacon and drain on paper towels. Reserve ¼ cup of the bacon drippings in the pan and return to medium heat. Sauté the diced onion in the drippings just until softened.

Add the vinegar mixture to the skillet and bring to a boil. Add the potatoes. Stir. Crumble the bacon and add along with the parsley. Toss gently to warm the potatoes. Add black pepper to taste and serve at once.

Wally's Potato Salad

Should feed 8 to 10

6 medium russet potatoes, peeled and cut into bite-sized pieces
⅓ cup vinegar
¼ cup olive oil
¼ cup mayonnaise
2 tablespoons sweet-pickle juice
1 tablespoon Dijon mustard
½ teaspoon sugar
½ teaspoon salt, plus more for salting cooking water
1 onion, diced
3 stalks celery, diced
4 hard-cooked eggs, chopped
½ cup chopped sweet pickles
2 cloves garlic, flattened, peeled and minced
2 teaspoons freshly ground black pepper
1 teaspoon dried dill weed
1 teaspoon paprika for garnish

Boil potatoes in salted water to cover until just fork-tender (almost al dente, not mushy). With a slotted spoon, remove potatoes to drain in a colander; then pour cooking liquid into a bowl and reserve to thin the salad later if necessary. Off the heat, put potatoes back into the pot to dry further; stir occasionally.

In a large bowl, whisk together vinegar, oil, mayo, pickle juice, mustard, sugar and salt.

Add onion, celery, eggs, pickles, garlic, black pepper and dill weed; gently stir to mix.

Add potatoes and mix thoroughly but gently. If salad looks too dry, add a little of the reserved water.

Taste for seasoning and adjust if necessary. Cover and refrigerate until chilled; then sprinkle with paprika and serve.

Skillet Cornbread

Should feed 6 to 8

3 eggs
¼ teaspoon sugar
1½ cups buttermilk
1½ cup flour
2 teaspoons baking powder
1½ teaspoons salt
½ teaspoon baking soda
1 cup yellow cornmeal
¼ cup melted butter
Canola oil for greasing skillet

Preheat oven to 400 degrees F.

In a large bowl, beat eggs with sugar until blended. Stir in buttermilk.

Into another bowl, sift together flour, baking powder, salt and baking soda. Stir in cornmeal and blend thoroughly.

Add flour-cornmeal mixture, a little at a time, to egg-buttermilk mixture, stirring to blend after each addition. Stir in melted butter and blend thoroughly.

Moisten a paper towel with oil and wipe the bottom and sides of a 10-inch cast-iron skillet to grease. Place skillet in preheated oven for 8 to 10 minutes to heat.

Remove heated skillet from oven and pour in batter. Bake for 30 minutes until light golden-brown on top.

Cut into wedges, pie-style, and serve with pinto beans or black-eyed peas, with plenty of sliced onion.

Desserts

Doris' Mayonnaise Cake

This was a dessert staple in our home when I was a kid. It was great with homemade ice cream after a big plate of barbecue. I guess this should have been called Miracle Whip Cake instead of Mayonnaise Cake, since it uses Miracle Whip Dressing (note that the Miracle Whip should be at room temperature; it's best to use an unopened jar that hasn't been refrigerated). My mother clipped the original recipe from the newspaper in the early '50's; she fiddled with it till it tasted right to her. Today my daughter, Kim, has mastered this fine dessert.

Should feed 8 to 10

Cake:

3 cups flour
1½ cups sugar
4½teaspoons cocoa (plus extra for dusting pans)
2¼ teaspoons baking soda
2¼ teaspoons baking powder
1½ cups cold water
3 teaspoons vanilla extract
6 drops black-walnut extract
12 ounces (1½ cups) Miracle Whip (use unopened room-temp jar)

Preheat oven to 325 degrees F.

Into a large mixing bowl, sift together flour, sugar, the 4½ teaspoons cocoa, baking soda and baking powder.

Stir in the remaining ingredients, in order listed. Mix with electric mixer until smooth.

Grease two 8-inch cake pans and dust with cocoa. Divide batter equally between pans. Bake in preheated 325-degree oven for 30 to 35 minutes. While cakes are baking, make icing:

Chocolate icing:
1 stick (8 tablespoons) butter
½ cup whole milk
2 cups sugar
½ cup cocoa
3 teaspoons vanilla extract
6 drops almond extract

In a saucepan on medium heat, melt butter; then add milk, sugar and cocoa. Stir until fully melted and combined. Bring to a boil and let boil for one minute only. Turn off heat and stir in vanilla and almond extracts.

Assembly:
Spread a little less than half the icing over bottom cake layer, place second cake layer on top and spread remaining icing on top and sides of cake, making sure to cover all the sides.

Ice Cream to the Power of Three ... Plus One

My sister, Kathy, serves this easy-to-make frozen treat often. Someone gave her the recipe years ago, and she tweaked it till she liked it. Matches perfectly with the Mayonnaise Cake.

Makes about a gallon

3 quarts half-and-half
3 cups sugar
3 teaspoons vanilla extract
1 tablespoon flour

Thoroughly mix ingredients. Chill for a couple of hours and then process according to instructions for your favorite ice cream maker.

Cobbler

If a Texas barbecue joint serves desserts, you can be pretty sure one of them will be cobbler. My sister, Kathy, has perfected the fine art of our mom's cobblers, and she has shared her recipes with me. There are two main schools of Texas cobblers, each with passionate adherents: those in which a biscuit-dough crust is rolled out and placed on top of the filling, like a piecrust, and those in which the crust is made from a batter that is poured into the bottom of the dish and rises through the filling to make a crust on top. This recipe is of the latter persuasion. You can use many kinds of fruit for the filling; the versions below are for peach and cherry. Whichever you use, this also goes great with the homemade ice cream.

Should feed 6 to 10

Batter:
½ cup milk (for the peach filling, my sister says, use evaporated milk)
½ cup sugar
½ cup flour
¼ cup butter, softened to room temperature, plus more for greasing baking dish
½ teaspoon salt
1 teaspoon baking powder

Preheat oven to 350 degrees F. Butter the inside of an 8-inch Pyrex baking dish.

In a mixing bowl, whisk together all ingredients until blended. Pour into prepared dish.

Peach filling:
15.5-oz. can of peaches in syrup, drained, ¼ cup of liquid reserved
1 tablespoon flour
¼ cup sugar
1 to 4 drops almond extract, to taste

In a bowl, mix fruit syrup with flour, whisking to blend. Stir in sugar and almond extract; mix thoroughly. Stir in peaches. Pour fruit mixture over batter in Pyrex dish.

Bake in preheated 350-degree oven 30 to 35 minutes, until browned on top. Serve with vanilla ice cream.

Cherry filling:
15.5-ounce can of tart pitted cherries, drained, ¼ cup of liquid reserved
1 tablespoon flour
1 cup sugar
1 to 4 drops black-walnut extract

In a bowl, mix fruit syrup with flour, whisking to blend. Stir in sugar and black walnut extract; mix thoroughly. Stir in cherries. Pour over batter.

Bake in preheated 350-degrees F oven 30 to 35 minutes, until browned on top. Serve with vanilla ice cream.

Princess Kathi's Cookies

Sometimes we are too full after barbecue to enjoy a big dessert. If I am lucky, my wife, Princess Kathi, has made some of her signature oatmeal cookies. I think this recipe started out as the one that used to be on the box of oatmeal, but Kathi has improved it. I am spoiled, so these are the only cookies I eat.

Makes 3 dozen to 4 dozen cookies

2 sticks (½ pound) butter, softened to room temperature
1 cup dark-brown sugar
½ cup granulated white sugar
2 teaspoons vanilla extract
3 eggs
1½ cups flour
1 teaspoon baking soda
1 teaspoon cinnamon
½ teaspoon salt
3 cups old-fashioned oatmeal (don't use instant or quick-cooking)
1 heaping cup raisins
½ cup pecan pieces
½ cup walnut pieces

Preheat oven to 350 degrees F.

In a large mixing bowl, using an electric mixer, beat butter together with both sugars until creamy. Beat in vanilla, then eggs; beat well to blend.

In a separate bowl, stir together flour, baking soda, cinnamon and salt. Add to butter-sugar mixture and blend thoroughly with mixer.

Stir in oats, raisins and nuts; mixing after each addition until blended.

Use a tablespoon to scoop and drop each cookie onto an ungreased cookie sheet. Bake 10 to 12 minutes at 350 until golden-brown. Cool on wire rack.

APPENDIX

Recommended Beverages

The beverage that comes to mind when I think of barbecue is beer. You can go the time-honored route and drink the brews that have been associated with barbecue in Texas for decades, or you can explore the exploding world of craft beers to find your best pairing. I've come up with some suggestions, but first I will say: Drink what you like. If it tastes good to you, then drink it!

Nostalgic beers

1. Lone Star: The beer geeks may be rolling their eyes, but Lone Star and Pearl top the nostalgic-beer list for Texas barbecue. For the last 50 years Lone Star signs have been a staple in barbecue joints around the state. Lone Star and Pearl are no longer Texas-owned, unlike our next beer on the list.

2. Shiner Bock: Here's another name synonymous with Texas barbecue. A pretty good beer to drink with barbecue, Shiner Bock is a light-bodied beer with dark color.

3. Miller High Life: This is on the nostalgic list for personal reasons: It was the first beer I drank with barbecue. At some point I realized that, on a hot day, an ice-cold beer tasted really good while I was barbecuing. All my friends drank Schlitz, Bud, Lone Star or Pearl, but Miller came in a bottle that was clear and had a different shape from the others, and I liked that. As beer goes, I've come to realize, it is not wonderful, but it was very satisfying for me for a number of years. I use it in my cooking and occasionally have a Miller while I am tending to the barbecue pit.

The real beer list

The beers below are really good with barbecue, and they are just a start. Some are bolder and heavier than others, so you can choose a beer in the style you like.

1. Pilsner Urquell: Here's my all-time favorite beer to have with barbecue. Plenty of flavor from a bright, light-tasting brew. You cannot go wrong drinking this beer with barbecue.

2. Sierra Nevada Pale Ale: My favorite American pale ale. These guys nailed this beer. This is my pick for barbecue-lovers who like a hoppy finish with slight citrus overtones. An easy-to-find, really nice beer.

3. Pedernales Brewing Company's Lobo: a great German-style pilsner from a Fredericksburg-based mainstay of Texas craft brewing.

4. Pedernales Brewing Company's Midnight Porter: For the lover of a more complex brew with a creamy finish. This is really good with spicy food.

5. The craft brewing explosion: So many craft beers are being produced now that there are hundreds to try. You can stick to regional offerings or range far and wide, but it always feels good to know you're drinking a Texas beer with your Texas barbecue.

Tequila

Before a barbecue dinner, we like to sip a chilly margarita. Just one of these will perk up your palate for the feast to follow.

Over the years, my circle of friends has endured my struggle in the quest for great food and beverages. One benefit they have received has been the Perfect Margarita. After years of research and countless hours of testing, I have achieved clarity. The secret recipe is below:

The Perfect Margarita

Remember, these are not like your mother's margaritas.

Kosher salt for glasses
1 part fresh squeezed lemon juice or Mexican lime juice (see note below)
1 part natural triple sec, brand of your choice
2 parts Herradura Silver Tequila (or your favorite)

Lightly coat the outside rim only of the desired number of 6-ounce glasses with kosher salt.

Pour all remaining ingredients into a shaker with fresh, unmelting ice cubes. Shake gently to thoroughly mix and chill. Pour into prepared glasses; can be served on the rocks or strained into glasses to serve straight up.

NOTE: If you cannot get Mexican limes, use lemons. Most limes in the market are Persian limes, and they can be very bitter at certain times of the year. Lemons, however, will not be bitter no matter what the season. This was a hard lesson for me to learn. Maria's, in Santa Fe, N.M., taught me this lesson, proving that you can teach an old dog new tricks. At first I did not believe this substitution would work, but I found that it works great. I still use a lime to moisten the rim of the glass for salt but now use lemons in all my margaritas.

Texas Barbecue Joints

The days when there was a local barbecue joint in most communities in Texas are behind us. Indeed, a few years ago I feared that the true Texas barbecue joint was fast becoming a thing of the past. Now, I think, there is hope, as this once-dying art is being brought back to life, maybe better than ever, by younger practitioners who revere wood and smoke. Still, many barbecuers are replacing the wood-fired pit with push-button, stainless-steel, gas-fired pits, marvels of modern technology and municipal mandates. Now, I am not saying these modern pits cannot produce barbecue, but there just is a difference between the end result of these automated, formatted devices and that of an old-fashioned wood pit. I will leave it to you, the reader, to decide: There are, after all, a few great old barbecue joints left in Texas, and you should visit them before they are gone.

Below is my list of my favorite barbecue joints in Texas, in no specific order. I believe that on any given day, any of these joints can produce the best barbecue in the world. They all have good days and better days; I have never experienced a bad day at any of them. I make no mention of sides or sauce, as they have little or no value for me: It is all about the meats.

1. Louie Mueller Barbecue, Taylor: This is, still, *THE* joint for me. I like everything about it. For barbecue ambiance, Louis Mueller's is the runaway winner. As soon as you step through the screen door, you know you have entered barbecue heaven. This joint looks like, feels like and smells like a Texas barbecue joint should. I got a tour of the pit on a past visit. It was fired with post oak (my favorite fuel), and it reminded me of a proud warrior. Though the original pit suffered from a fire and has since been replaced, I am happy to report that the meats are still outstanding. Plenty of heat with just enough smoke makes for perfect barbecue. The fatty end of the brisket, cut "inside-out," with a piece of bread wrapped around it, is sublime. The sausage, regular or jalapeño, is very good. The pork ribs are cooked just right, and the simple salt and pepper rub they use on their meats lets the flavor of the pork shine. On Saturday there are fine beef ribs, with plenty of spice from loads of black pepper. 206 W. Second St., 512-352-6206, www.louiemuellerbarbecue.com

2. Black's Barbecue, Lockhart: Since 1932, Black's has been serving up great Texas barbecue. It seems to get better every time I visit. I always go for the brisket and sausage, but my trusty sidekick swears by the spareribs. I love this joint. 215 N. Main St., 512-398-2712, www.blacksbbq.com

3. Snow's BBQ, Lexington: Open only on Saturdays. Get there early (the line starts forming before they open at 8 a.m.), because they always sell out. Nice brisket, pork, ribs and sausage. Tootsie Tomanetz has been cooking barbecue for more than 49 years and still does an excellent job at Snow's. 516 Main St., 979-542-8189, www.snowsbbq.com

4. Smitty's Market, Lockhart: You will probably have to wait in line here, but it will be worth it. This joint started out as Kreuz Market in the early 1900s, and Smitty's opened here after a split in the family business in the late 1990s. The same care and basic attention to detail exists in Smitty's as it did when this was Kreuz. These old pits, stoked with post oak, on a good day put out some of the best brisket, beef clod, sausage and pork ribs in the state. The sausage is just about the best you can find. Here again, nothing but salt and pepper goes on the meat. They tend to cook at a higher temperature than most other joints, but the results are very good, a little less smoky than some. 208 S. Commerce St., 512-398-9344, www.smittysmarket.com

5. Kreuz Market, Lockhart: After the family business split up in 1999, these guys opened a big new joint at the edge of town. The new digs don't mean new ways of doing things, though. The meats (beef, pork and sausage) are cooked with post oak and salt and pepper. On a great day, this can be really fine barbecue. I do love the sausage. 619 N. Colorado St., 512-398-2361, www.kreuzmarket.com

6. City Market, Luling: Things here have remained constant for the last five decades. Great barbecue brisket, pork ribs and sausage come off the post-oak-fired pit as a work of art, proving once again that simple is best. 633 E. Davis St., 830-875-9019

7. Cooper's Old Time Pit Bar-B-Que, Llano: Cooper's always has the most distinctive aroma when you walk up to the pits. Burning mesquite down to embers allows them to get a great flavor without any bitterness, which is sometimes evident in low-and-slow barbecue cooked with mesquite. A large assortment of meats — cabrito, pork chops, top sirloin, prime rib, brisket, beef and pork ribs, chicken, sausage — allows you take your pick right off the pit. The best assortment and quality are always found early in the day: Arriving before they open at 10 a.m. can reward you with some great Texas barbecue. 604 W. Young St., 325-247-5713, www.coopersbbq.com

8. Franklin Barbecue, Austin: Maybe the best barbecue in Texas. If not, they are somewhere at the very top of the list. The great barbecue is diminished only by the incredible wait. I got there two hours before they opened and sat down to eat three hours later. I believe I'll leave this one for the young folks to enjoy; at my age, the old saying "Is the juice worth the squeeze?" keeps crossing my mind at Franklin's. Maybe if I lived somewhere outside Texas or didn't cook barbecue at home year 'round, I might be more inclined to wait in a long line for it. You can order a whole brisket, chilled and vacuum-sealed, and just walk in and pick it up, though, and when I heard about their plans to add a to-go window, that sounded good to me. 900 E. 11th St., 512-653-1187, www.franklinbarbecue.com

9. The rest: There are many new barbecue joints popping up in Texas, and it is certainly exciting to see the young folks take barbecue seriously. This once-dying art is being brought back to life, maybe better than ever. Find your favorite joint and meat and reward yourself often. Texas barbecue has brought me tremendous joy over the last 60 years.

Weights and Measures

1 tablespoon = 3 teaspoons
1 fluid ounce = 2 tablespoons
¼ cup = 4 tablespoons = 2 fluid ounces
1 cup = 16 tablespoons = 8 fluid ounces
1 pint = 2 cups
1 quart = 2 pints = 4 cups
1 gallon = 4 quarts = 16 cups

Metric conversion

1 teaspoon = 5 milliliters
1 tablespoon = 15 milliliters
1 fluid ounce = 34 milliliters
½ cup = 120 milliliters

Weight

1 ounce = 28 grams
1 pound = 454 grams/.454 kilograms (approximately ½ kg)
1 kilogram = 2.2 pounds

The Author

Chef Wally, aka John Lopez, grew up in Houston's Near North Side in the 1950s. His mother was a great cook and passed some of her special knowhow to him.

Wally was a professional musician for five years and a mechanical engineer for 10 years before moving to Southern California to open gourmet kitchen stores, a cooking school and a "fresh-only" catering company. A self-taught chef, he specialized in "glorified peasant food." His culinary studies included the foods of South Louisiana, India, Thai, Vietnam and China; country foods from France and Italy; regional Mexican and Tex-Mex; and, of course, Texas foods and Texas barbecue.

Chef Wally sold his business interest in California in 1989 to return to Texas as a consultant to the retail gourmet trade. He and his wife, Kathi, then started and operated a small gourmet marketing company.

They now reside in Fredericksburg, Texas, and are proud members of Team Der Küchen Laden, helping run the finest kitchen shop in the great state of Texas.

Chef Wally can be reached via email: wallypez@hotmail.com

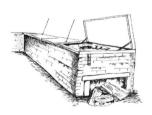

Other great regional cookbooks from Great Texas Line Press

Sweet Southern: A Heritage of Beloved Desserts

"Anyone looking for a collection of traditional recipes – cakes, cobblers, pies – will want to check it out." –*The Tennesseean*. "The book's budget friendly price makes it the perfect item to keep on hand for last minute gifts." –*Houston Chronicle*. "This sweet little book offers the basic, best recipes for pies, pralines that helped make us what we are." –*Port Arthur News*. "Offers the South's favorite sweets!" –*Baton Rouge Advocate*. 88 pages. ISBN 1-892588-06-4. $5.95.

Salsa! Salsa! Salsa!

Crystal Walls' guide to making salsas for every occasion, to grace any cuisine. More than 70 varieties ensures you'll never run out of fresh ideas to serve up. "Hottest book on the shelf" – *Fort Worth Star-Telegram*. "This pocket sized book will surprise and delight you with its 75 creative and unique salsa recipes." –*Amazon* reader review. 88 pages. ISBN 1-892588-05-6. $5.95.

Championship Chili

A guide to making chili, using recipes that swept top honors at the leading two national cook-offs. Includes a veteran competitor-judge's secrets on making a winning bowl of blessedness. "Best darn chili book in either direction of the Pecos" – *Big Bend Sentinel*. A portion of proceeds benefits the Big Bend Educational Foundation. 80 pages. ISBN 1-892588-03-X. $5.95.

Texas Church Supper and Family Reunion Cookbook

Veteran cooks Dolores Runyon and Dona Mularkey combined their favorite recipes into a little 84-page book chock full of delicious ideas for that family reunion or church potluck. –*San Angelo Standard-Times* ISBN 1-892588-07-2. $5.95.

Tex Mex 101

"From family favorites to gourmet creations, recipes from Texans who know" –*Sherman-Denison Herald-Democrat*. This handy guide makes genuine Texan-Mexican cuisine accessible to any kitchen. Includes fajitas, enchiladas, tres leches cake and Chef Dean Fearing's famous Turtle Mansion Tortilla Soup. 80 pages. ISBN 1-892588-02-1. $5.95.

Visit *www.greattexasline.com* to survey all of our scrumptious titles.